THE SEA \
BETWEEN
TEIGNMOUTH & DAWLISH
by A.R. Kingdom

ARK PUBLICATIONS
(RAILWAYS)

First published in 2008 by ARK PUBLICATIONS (RAILWAYS), an imprint of
FOREST PUBLISHING, Woodstock, Liverton, Newton Abbot, Devon TQ12 6JJ

British Library Cataloguing in Publication Data
A catalogue record for this book is available from the British Library
ISBN 978–1–873029–15–2

Dawlish seafront in its heyday during the 1920s, viewed towards the west. Note the
ice cream sellers, one at the foot of the steps and the other with a Walls' 'Stop me
and buy one' tricycle just to the right of the charabanc.

C.N. Jamson of Empire View Productions, Doncaster
(Courtesy of Mike Willis)

ARK PUBLICATIONS (RAILWAYS)
Editorial, layout and design by:
Mike Lang

Typeset by:
Carnaby Typesetting, Torquay, Devon TQ1 1EG

Printed and bound in Great Britain by:
Wotton Printers Limited, Newton Abbot, Devon TQ12 4PJ

Cover photographs:

Front – Long after the demise of steam for public transport in the 1960s, steam
specials still frequent the sea wall. In this photograph, taken on Sunday,
31st August 2003, No. 7802 *Bradley Manor* is seen passing Eastcliff with
the 9.08 a.m. Bristol Temple Meads to Kingswear 'Torbay Express'.

Bernard Mills

Back – 'Hall' class 4–6–0 No. 6981 *Marbury Hall,* with a 'down' express, battles
against the elements as it passes through Dawlish during a very stormy day
in March 1960.

PREFACE

This book, number 6 in the popular 'Railway ARKives' series, is based almost wholly on a photographic record of the railway between Teignmouth and Dawlish (including Dawlish Warren), which was compiled by three generations of the Chapman family. Starting with William James Chapman, who established the firm in Dawlish which later became known as Chapman & Son, their combined efforts stretched from the 1860s to 1967 and resulted in the production of one of the county's largest photographic collections of scenes and events.

Some years ago I was fortunate in acquiring, from Bernard Chapman, the entire railway collection and its associated postcard production equipment. Prior to then, and from the early 1900s, the 'Chapman & Son' photographs were reproduced as postcards, so they have now been in the public domain for many years. They have also appeared singly or severally in numerous publications but, in spite of this, I make no apologies for bringing together a comprehensive collection of their pictures of this beautiful part of the South Devonshire coastline. In so doing, it portrays a century of local railway history and, at the same time, serves as a fitting tribute to the Chapman family.

The poem featured in the appendix is by the late T.W.E. Roche, MA and is included because, to my mind, it is one of the best railway poems I have encountered. It typifies the scene in the 1920s of a small boy watching an express train going along the sea wall as he paddles in the sea with his bucket and spade. The metre even picks up the rattle of the train's wheels as it thunders past!

The 29xx 'Saint' class locomotives were the workhorses of the time, preceding the more famous 'Kings', 'Castles' and 'Halls' of later years: No. 2907, *Lady Disdain,* was built in May 1906, named in April 1907 and finally withdrawn from service in July 1933.

T.W.E. Roche was passionate about trains, especially those of the Great Western Railway. Holding high office, he was well placed to become an anchorman during the very early days of railway preservation in the 1960s. As a member of the Great Western Society he became a friend of mine and also of Bryan Gibson, who has contributed greatly to this and all my previous books.

A. R. Kingdom
Yealmpton
Devon

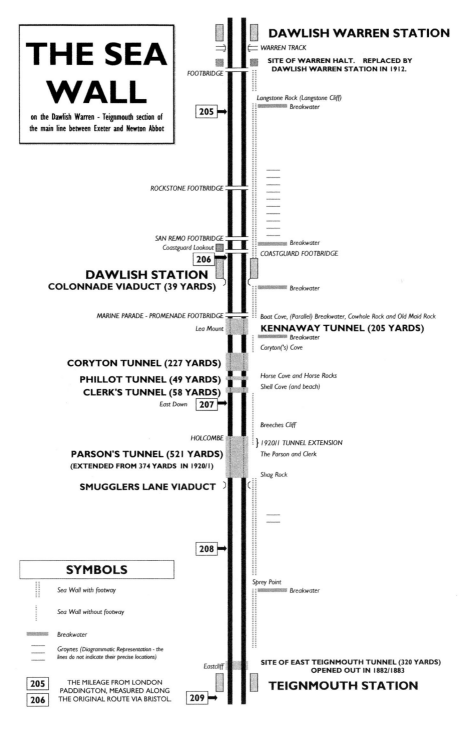

THE SEA WALL

on the Dawlish Warren - Teignmouth section of the main line between Exeter and Newton Abbot

DAWLISH WARREN STATION

WARREN TRACK

SITE OF WARREN HALT. REPLACED BY DAWLISH WARREN STATION IN 1912.

FOOTBRIDGE

Langstone Rock (Langstone Cliff)
Breakwater

`205`

ROCKSTONE FOOTBRIDGE

SAN REMO FOOTBRIDGE
Coastguard Lookout
Breakwater
COASTGUARD FOOTBRIDGE

`206`

DAWLISH STATION
COLONNADE VIADUCT (39 YARDS)

Breakwater

MARINE PARADE - PROMENADE FOOTBRIDGE
Boat Cove, (Parallel) Breakwater, Cowhole Rock and Old Maid Rock
Lea Mount
KENNAWAY TUNNEL (205 YARDS)
Breakwater
Coryton('s) Cove

CORYTON TUNNEL (227 YARDS)
PHILLOT TUNNEL (49 YARDS)
Horse Cove and Horse Rocks
CLERK'S TUNNEL (58 YARDS)
Shell Cove (and beach)
East Down `207`

Breeches Cliff

HOLCOMBE
} 1920/1 TUNNEL EXTENSION
PARSON'S TUNNEL (521 YARDS)
The Parson and Clerk
(EXTENDED FROM 374 YARDS IN 1920/1)

Shag Rock

SMUGGLERS LANE VIADUCT

`208`

SYMBOLS

Sprey Point
Breakwater

Sea Wall with footway

Sea Wall without footway

Breakwater

Groynes (Diagrammatic Representation - the lines do not indicate their precise locations)

Eastcliff
SITE OF EAST TEIGNMOUTH TUNNEL (320 YARDS)
OPENED OUT IN 1882/1883

`205` THE MILEAGE FROM LONDON
`206` PADDINGTON, MEASURED ALONG
THE ORIGINAL ROUTE VIA BRISTOL.

`209` **TEIGNMOUTH STATION**

4

CONTENTS

ACKNOWLEDGEMENTS

The author is indebted to the following in the production of this book.

Bryan Gibson (map and tickets); Mike Lang; Bernard Mills; Mike Willis.

(Photographs are by Chapman & Son of Dawlish except where individually acknowledged.)

INTRODUCTION

The popular conception of the coastline between Teignmouth and Dawlish is of a fine summer's day with families on holiday strolling along the sea wall or swimming in the sea, their picnics laid out with their towels on the red sand.

My first glimpses of the scene, however, were totally different – to the extreme, in fact! It was early in the Second World War and we had been bombed out during the Blitz on Plymouth. At the time my father was a non-combatant naval officer called back from retirement to oversee the delivery of ships for the Royal Navy from the Clydeside shipyards in Scotland, and he was taking my mother and me back with him to Glasgow for a short break, away from the chaos at home.

The date was actually sometime during November 1941, when I was ten years old, and as our train ran through Teignmouth Station and out onto the sea wall towards Dawlish the sky was leaden; it had become a dark and dreary afternoon. Consequently, the front and beaches were deserted, and all that could be seen was barbed wire and invasion obstacles adorning the shoreline and pillboxes sited at strategic points adjacent to the mouths of the tunnels. Our train, meanwhile, was packed, and the general mood of the passengers was as grey as the sea and equally foreboding, despite the fact that the early invasion scares of 1940 had passed with the success of the Battle of Britain. Even having the lights switched on inside the train did little to improve matters, as the bulbs were painted with a blue translucent paint in order to prevent the lights from being seen by enemy aircraft!

Now, some 66 years later, the threat of war and consequent attack is but a dimming recollection in the minds of my generation. Nevertheless, the threat of invasion is still very much with us, the only difference being that it is from the sea itself, which continues, relentlessly, to erode the soft sandstone cliffs and shore. It is, in fact, for this very reason that throughout the 160-plus years of its existence the sea wall has seldom been out of the news, especially in more recent times with the onset of global warming and rising sea levels.

At this point it is, perhaps, interesting to reflect that in the late 1930s no less than three alternative inland deviations for the railway line were proposed and that even an Act of Parliament was passed. However, escalating costs and the onset of the Second World War put paid to this venture and the status quo remains to this day. This, in turn, means that if the sea wall ever did succumb to the elements and the line had to be closed the effect on the sustainable economy of places such as the seaside towns of Teignmouth and Dawlish, not to mention that of the South West as a whole, would be catastrophic. It only remains for me to say, therefore, that whatever the cost of keeping it open, this vital West Country link and the truly scenic gem into which it is set must be preserved for the well-being and enjoyment of both the present and future generations alike.

A.R. Kingdom

March 2008

✱ ✱ ✱ ✱ ✱

THE SEA WALL

A pictorial survey

Teignmouth

The original South Devon Railway station at Teignmouth, looking westwards and showing the baulk road and wooden buildings (c.1893).

Author's collection

The sea wall 'under attack' as an unidentified 'up' train approaches Sprey Point (c.1896).

Friths

'Castle' class 4–6–0 No. 5047 *Earl of Dartmouth* passes under Eastcliff viaduct with an 'up' express in July 1947.

Lens of Sutton

'King' class 4–6–0 No. 6003 *King George IV* seen running westwards of Sprey Point with the 'down' 'Limited' on 18th July 1947.

Lens of Sutton

Nos. 5011 *Tintagel Castle* and 6001 *King Edward VII,* on a 'down' express to Plymouth, seen from Shaldon Bridge leaving Teignmouth and running alongside the Teign estuary (c.1950s).

Author's collection

'County' class 4–6–0 No. 1015 *County of Gloucester* heads out of Teignmouth on an 'up' train (c.1956).

'Hall' class 4–6–0 No. 6987 *Shervington Hall,* on a 'down' express, approaches Sprey Point on 20th April 1957.

Lens of Sutton

'Castle' class 4–6–0 No. 5074 *Denbigh Castle* leaves Teignmouth with the 'up' 'Torbay Express' on 23rd April 1957.

Lens of Sutton

Holcombe

A '45xx' class 2–6–2T, No. 4575, on an Exeter to Teignmouth local train at Holcombe (c.1933).

An unidentified 'Hall' class 4–6–0 emerges from the tunnel at Coryton Cove with an 'up' train (c.1950s).

Another of the 'Hall' class locos working hard as it accelerates past Smugglers Lane Beach with an 'up' express (c.1950s).

An ex-SR 'West Country' class 4–6–2, No. 34029 *Lundy,* heading for Teignmouth with a 'down' passenger train whilst on crew training (c.1954).

A distant view of the railway at Shell Cove, with a 'down' train being hauled by a '51xx' class 2–6–2T locomotive (c.1957).

A bird's-eye view of a 'Castle' class 4–6–0 soon after having emerged from Parson's tunnel with a 'down' express (c.late 1950s).

An unidentified 'Hall' class 4–6–0 emerges from Parson's tunnel with a 'down' express. Note the permanent way hut, the lengths of replacement rail between the rails of the 'down' track and also the wartime pillbox to the right of the tunnel (c.1960).

Dawlish

The original South Devon Railway station at Dawlish with its staff (c.1870). Constructed of timber, this was destroyed by a fire in 1873 and replaced by the present-day structure.

Another, roadside, view of the original station at Dawlish. The tall structure directly behind it is the chimney of the atmospheric railway's pumping house (c.1870).

A view of the single, broad-gauge, track at Dawlish, looking eastwards towards the original station and the atmospheric railway's pumping house beyond. The photograph also shows a SDR 4–4–0ST on a 'down' train of six, four-wheeled, coaches and, in the foreground, a disc and crossbar signal. Note the bathing machines on the beach (c.1870).

The broad-gauge track at Dawlish as seen from Marine Parade, looking westwards towards Lea Mount (c.1880s).

A view from Lea Mount of the GWR station at Dawlish; again, broad-gauge track is visible, but semaphore signals now replace the former disc and crossbar type (c.1890).

A summertime view of the broad-gauge track at Dawlish, looking towards Lea Mount and with Colonnade viaduct in the foreground, to the right (c.1890).

The eastern end of Kennaway tunnel, below Lea Mount, showing cross-sleeper and mixed gauge track. This was one of the sections of SDR track so laid before gauge conversion began (c.1891).

Narrowing the gauge at the western end of Dawlish Station during the weekend of 21st/22nd May 1892 (sawn-off pieces of the old baulk road transoms lie in the 'six foot').

Dawlish Station with a 'Badminton' class 4–4–0 on a 'down' express of clerestory coaches (c.1900).

A 'Bulldog' class 4–4–0, *Avalon,* on an 'up' express at Coryton Cove. Originally numbered 3332, this engine was later renumbered 3320 (c.1900).

Author's collection

GWR loco No. 100 *William Dean* leaves Dawlish with a 'down' express. The leading coach is a Travelling Post Office vehicle (c.1906).

GWR steam railcar No. 38 arrives at Dawlish Station on an 'up' local working (c.1908).

A panoramic view from Lea Mount of Marine Parade and the station at Dawlish. It shows an 'up' passenger train headed by a 'Saint' class 4–6–0, and a 'down' train waiting at the station (c.1910).

A '2301' class 0–6–0 ('Dean Goods') approaches Dawlish Station with a 'down' goods train (c.1920).

A view of Dawlish Station from the north, showing the goods yard with various types of wagons in the sidings (c.1921).

A 'Dean Goods' employed on shunting operations just beyond the entrance to the goods yard. Note the many wooden groynes stretching into the sea in order to combat erosion (c.1920s).

A view of Marine Parade, with a 'Saint' class 4–6–0 heading a 'down' express. The leading coach is seen to be a clerestory type (c.1924).

An 0–6–0PT, No. 5760, seen arriving at Dawlish with a 'down' goods on 23rd August 1937.

No. 6007 *King William III* on an 'up' 'Limited' at Coryton Cove (c.1938).

R.S. Carpenter

Dawlish Station, looking eastwards (c.1950s).

The view from Lea Mount as 'Hall' class 4–6–0 No. 6994 *Baggrave Hall,* with a Torbay portion of a 'down' express, steams away to the west (c.1950s). Note that the large steps built into the sea wall, which are clearly visible in earlier photographs, have, by now, been removed.

A view of Dawlish Station and goods yard from the Coastguard House, looking westwards (c.1953). Note the changes since the lower photograph appearing on page 21 was taken, in particular the extended platforms (dating from 1934) and the wooden groynes stretching into the sea.

A view from Boat Cove of a 'Hall' class 4–6–0 and its train heading westwards towards Kennaway tunnel (c.1955).

The popular view from Lea Mount shows No. 6929 *Whorlton Hall* with a 'down' express during the late 1950s.

ROUGH SEA. DAWLISH   28447

A British Railways class '9F' 2-10-0 passing Dawlish with a heavy 'down' freight train during the severe gales of December 1962.

No. 6974 *Bryngwoyn Hall* passing Dawlish with a 'down' goods, 19th January 1963.
G.V. Lendon

A 'down' stopping service DMU is photographed from the public park as it passes over Colonnade viaduct on its journey westwards (late 1960s).
Bernard Mills

Dawlish Warren

There were no facilities for passengers at Dawlish Warren until the opening of Warren Halt in 1905. This was situated about 200 yards to the south of the later station, and is depicted above with GWR steam railcar No. 44 stood alongside the 'down' platform whilst on a local working.

The platforms at Warren Halt were lengthened in 1906 and additional accommodation was provided during the following year. It was then renamed Warren Platform, as shown in this photograph taken with a 'down' train awaiting the 'off' (c.1907).

Author's collection

Another view of Warren Platform, this time on a busy day during the summer of 1911. By now a new passenger station was under construction (part of the new 'down' platform can just be seen in the distance) and work was also progressing on a new goods yard with two sidings in the area to the west (left) of the 'up' platform.

Lens of Sutton

A view of the 'new' station at Dawlish Warren as a 'Saint' class 4–6–0 arrives with an 'up' passenger train of mixed stock (c.1914).

Additional sea defences being built at Dawlish Warren during the early 1920s. Note the long spur of siding laid to offload stone for the purpose.

A view from Langstone Cliff as a '2251' class 0–6–0 leaves Dawlish Warren Station with a portion of a 'down' express. Note the sea wall defences, now complete with a pathway and wall, and the sleepers from the temporary siding lying beside the track (c.1950).

APPENDIX

'Lady Disdain'

I stood in the shallows just west of the tunnel
The cliff seemed to shake with the oncoming train
Then out dashed a vision of copper-topped funnel,
Black smokebox, green boiler, my 'Lady Disdain'.

Two thousand nine hundred and seven her number –
How often I stood in that Devonshire sea
All lukewarm and still in its midsummer slumber
To wave as her enginemen whistled to me!

The more I behold her the greater my pining
Smoke flying behind her along the sea wall
Her driving wheels spinning, her safety valve shining
My Lady now had me completely in thrall.

"Oh, please take me with you to far-away cities
Whose names I can read on your dining car's roof!"
The Lady just whistled in scorn, for she pitied
Me not and her smoke was a silent reproof.

"Presumptuous fellow! to travel behind me,"
She shrieked as she plunged in the tunnel again
"I've gone and I'll warrant you never will find me!"
The cliff echoed back to my 'Lady Disdain'.

From that evening forward I never beheld her
Though I sought her intently all over the line
At Old Oak, at Tyseley, at Canton, at Laira
And found every other Great Western 'Two Nine'.

Let this be a warning to all who would travel
To hark to the carriage wheels' mocking refrain
Don't try and solve secrets you cannot unravel
Or harness your heart to a 'Lady Disdain'!

T.W.E. Roche

BIBLIOGRAPHY

There have been so many books published that include reference to the main line of railway between Teignmouth and Dawlish that I have restricted the entries in this Bibliography to just four that I have found particularly useful as sources of reference.

Exeter – Newton Abbot, A Railway History, Peter Kay (Platform 5 Publishing Ltd, 1993)

An Historical Survey of Selected Great Western Stations, Layouts and Illustrations, Volume Two, R. H. Clark (Oxford Publishing Co., 1979)

Rails along the Sea Wall, Peter Kay (Platform 5 Publishing Ltd, 1990)

Through the Window (Great Western Railway Company, 1939 – Peninsula Press reprint, 1994)

✳ ✳ ✳ ✳ ✳

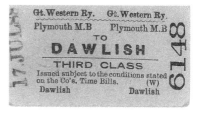